Decimos
We Say

2019 DECAs

DECA

Thank you to all the Sponsors of the 2019 DECAs

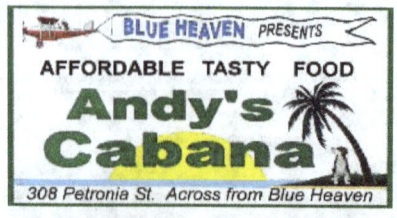

Decimos - We Say is published by Elegant Publications Company, LLC
2019

Publisher: JD Adler

editorial board:
Edgardo Alvarado-Vazquez
Vicki Boguszewski
Kalo Clarke
Flower Conroy

Copyright 2019 Elegant Publications Company.
All Rights Reserved. Authors and artists retain all rights to their work unless specified otherwise.

ISBN: 9781087812717

Decimos (We Say) was born during the turbulent summer of 2017, the culmination of years of projects, dreams and vague imaginations. The title was chosen to reflect our goal to provide every talented writer in the Keys, published or amateur, access to a venue where they can play with their ideas, share them with their community, and maybe launch something more. The Keys are bursting with stories true and imagined; it is time we began to record them.

Our editorial board consists of local writers with experience and accolades as professional writers, artists and editors; Edgardo Alvarado-Vazquez, Vicki Boguszewski, Kalo Clarke and the former Poet Laureate of Key West, Flower Conroy. After two editors have seen every submission, with all names removed, I weigh in on any disparate opinions, and our selection is made. We wish to showcase as wide a spectrum of the quality writers in our community as possible.

The Keys have long been a melting pot of the absurd; fisherman and transvestites, carpenters and exhibitionists, art galleries and live aboards, hotel chains and environmentalists, snowbirds and chugs, bartenders and, well, other bartenders, all gathered together on a narrow archipelago in the sub-tropics. Traditionally, the arts reflect the culture they call home. I am excited to see what we produce.

I hope you enjoy what follows.

Thank you,

J.D. Adler
Publisher of Decimos - We Say
Elegant Publications Company, LLC
Key West, Florida

Contents

Corkscrew
Tod Perry • Key West • Issue #13

How Information Technology Has Made My Life Sooo Much Better
Scaly Galey • Tavernier • Issue #13

Thunder Goddess
P Pattent Tiffany • Key West • Issue #14

Holes in My Head
Sheri Lohr • Key West • Issue #14

Worms on the Brain
William "Bucky" Montgomery • Key West • Issue #14

Plead
Vinny Scotts • Key West • Issue #15

Gangus Hausenfluck
Jelena Sanchez • Key West • Issue #15

Heist by the Local Dinosaur
Christina Tong • Key West • Issue #15

Plover Promise
P Patten Tiffany • Key West • Issue #16

A Little Pain in the Butt Never Hurt Anyone
Alexandra Hope • Key West • Issue #16

Corkscrew
Tod Perry
Key West
Issue #13

He walks to his room
sees down a hall
himself in himself
smaller smaller
mirror in mirror
unsure which image
in what mirror he is.

At that moment shows
in a pace that now slows
him worn by distractions
and the weight of his day,

Sinks down into bed
at first to the left
and then on the right
to spin in a darkness
that turns into dawn,
and with one final whirl,
twists himself up,
upright, erect.

How Information Technology Has Made My Life Sooo Much Better
Scaly Galey
Tavernier
Issue #13

When I was a girl, body builder Charles Atlas would show how strong he was by tearing up a telephone book. Now a 90 lb. weakling could do it.

Have you seen a Florida Keys telephone book in the last couple of years? It is thin and anemic. The pages that aren't the color of hepatitis are anorexic, and my name is not in them. They are only for businesses unwilling to spring for the extra cost of a listing in the yellow pages. I was surprised to find that even many of the most well-known businesses are not listed. We live in Monroe County, Florida where it's all about tourism and fishing. I tried looking up World Wide Sportsman, the famous fishing boutique. It was not there. Maybe it's under one of their affiliates: Bass Pro Shops. No. Offshore Fishing. Nope. Outdoor World. Not a chance.

I picked up my black landline telephone and dialed 411 for the information operator. For a long time now, this system has been completely automated. No more operators. Not even any supervisors. In fact, there is no living human being anywhere there. The world could end, and it would still go on forever.

Blip blip sounds, followed by chimes. Then a socio-politically correct, gender-neutral robotic sing-song voice (probably programmed in the Philippines) comes over the telephone.

"AT&T Directory Assistance. Please say a city and state or say search by number."

Me: Islamorada, Florida.

"Eez-lay-mor-ay-day, Flor-ee-day. If that's not right say go back. What are you looking for? A business or a residence?"

Me: Uhhh...business.

"What is the business you want?"

Me: World Wild Sportsman.

"World Parrot Mission. Is that right? If not, say go back."

Me: No, go back.

"I am sorry. If that is not your number, say go back."

Me: Go back.

"What is your listing, please?"
Me: World Wide Sportsman.
"World's Purfitt Toe Rings. Is that right?"
Me: Oh, hell no!
"I am sorry. If that's not right, say go back."
Me: Go back.
"What is your listing?"
Me: World. Wide. Sportsman.
"World Wide Sportsman in Eez-lay-mor-ay-day. Is that right?"
Me, filling up with hopeful excitement: Yes. Yes! YES!!!
"I am sorry. We were unable to find your number. Would you like the number of another business?"
I am stunned. I don't say anything.
"Just say which one you want:
One. Iguana Be Gone. (blip)
Two. Gunky's Crane Service. (blip)
Three. Windy Day Plumbing. (blip)
Four. Octopuses Garden & Landscape. (blip)
Five. Eez-lay-mor-ay-day Dry Cleaners. (blip)
Six. Froggys Fitness in Tev-yen-ay." (blip)
(Our rob-o-voice must have been coached in English by a French Canadian.
"Seven. Critterdoc House Calls on Beeg Peen Key. (blip)
Eight. Woody's. (blip)
Nine. Scuba-do Dive Charters. (blip)
Ten. Scooby's Gourmet Popcorn. (blip)
Just say the one you want. You can also say 'none of them. Or repeat the list again'."
Me: I come to, and bang the dumb phone smartly on the table.
"First Baptist Church of Key Largo, where..." Bzzz, pop! Staticky sound. "...First State Bank in Key West...bzzz, pop...where Jesus saves...bzzz pop! Jesus Rodriquez sewer pipe connections and septic tank demolition. Enos Mitchell septic tanks.—tweet—that number has been disconnected."
Me: I lay my head on the table. I just want to go fishing...
"I have Gaitor-Baiter in Coopertown cane poles, live worms, crickets and air-boat rentals. Would you like that number?"
Me: I just need to get away, I mutter.
"Bobby Joe's crawdad catching and catfish noodling tours in Valdosta, Georgia. Would you like that number?"
Me: Far, far away...

"One moment, please, I will connect you with the ATT&T international long-distance operator. Exorbitant rates may apply."

Me: head still on table, I cock an eyebrow.

"Yah? Zees ees Vladivostok operator. I put you tru to Vladivostok Beluga Whale and Sturgeon stripping and caviar tasting Adventures. You will be billed 2,309.96 rubles or $34.82 USD per minute.

Me: Nyet, I reply.

My regular operator comes back on line. "I have World Wide Sportsman International Travel Fishing Adventures and Outfitters. Would you like that number?"

Me: I lift my head off the table. Yes, please!

"The number is blah blah blah-blah blah blah-blah blah-blah blah. If you stay on the line, I will connect you for a charge of 78 cents."

Me: I perk up. It's actually ringing! My heart is pounding in my chest.

Then I am tag teamed by her robot cousins, R2-D2 and C-3PO.

Errrr—eee—EEEE "If you wish to place a call, hang up and try again."

Me: I hook the telephone cord around my jaw and pull down to prevent profanities from coming out of my mouth because it's not ladylike and clearly a violation of FCC rules. I could get arrested by Robocop.

Me: OK, AT&T, I've got your number! Why can't you get mine???

I make like a pirate: ARRRGGHHH!!!! With my cutlass-like filleting knife I sever the land-line. ATT&T's last, dying voice was, "I am sor-rry we could not help youuu...."

I'm grabbing my hard-copy Webster's Dictionary. How do you spell "psychiatrist?"

And you darn well better not tell me to use Spell-Check!

My twelve-year-old granddaughter enters the room. "Grammy, it sounds like you're having a bad time with that telephone. Why don't you try my cellphone? I take it gingerly from her hand, wondering if this is the kind that blows up airplanes when its battery-made-in-China goes bananas.

"Just press the round button in the center at the bottom to turn it on."

I do so, the face lights up with the Samsung logo and, after a mo-

Decimos - We Say
2019 Price Sheet

1/4 page = $150/issue (3 months)
Full Page = $500/issue (3 months)

Decimos - We Say is a quarterly magazine. Ads purchased will run in print & digital version as well as on our website for the duration of the issue.

For more info:
JD Adler at contact@epcopress.com

Sample Full Page Ad

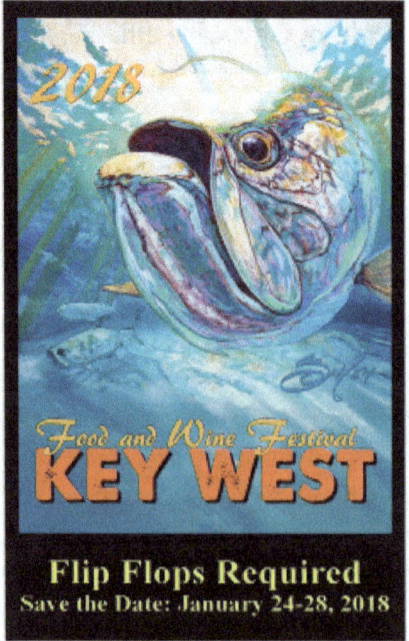

Sample 1/4 Page Ads

ment reminiscent of NBC's chimes, it's blissfully quiet. A flash of what my granddaughter calls "icons". No! Wait! It wants to give me breaking sports news. (I hate sports.) A picture of a kitten. Then advertisements. I hate ads! Finally, soothing "wallpaper" of a mountain scene with a placid lake in the foreground. I swipe right as indicated to a field of weird little icons. I have no idea why they're there. Or what they're for. Or what they do. I swipe furiously—more icons appear. Lower right corner a group of white dots that says "apps." I touch that—and millions more little pictures appear on the screen. The more I swipe, the more they appear! They're multiplying by the second! Is there no end to them? I swipe faster. They're shaking their tiny little fists or whatever at me. They begin a jiggle dance. "Ehhhh!" I scream. This thing is vibrating in my hand like it's going to explode.

"Gurrrgh!" Sound it makes. Sound I make. Sound the kitchen disposal makes.

Granddaughter's mouth makes an "O", and her face goes white.

"Grammy, why'd you destroy my cellphone?" Tears are running down her cheeks.

"It's OK, sweetie, I'll get you another. She's still crying. "All right, all right, I'll buy you an X-box or a PlayStation (whatever they are)." Instantly her tears dry up and she's grinning like a rabid raccoon.

After shopping, we go to the movies. Before the main feature, are previews. Before that, there are ADVERTISEMENTS!!! $15 I paid for tickets, and still we are made to endure more ads.

The lights dim. We are told to turn off our cellphones. No problem there.

Thunder Goddess
P Pattent Tiffany
Key West
Issue #14

Hear her mighty song
crack and roll
to emphasize
a point.

She is a senator
a healer
a mother of lighting
who blazes the night sky

to open the dark below
heave up old highways
scorch old earth clean.

Avenger, unleashing
bolts and hail
to tainted earth.

"Come, Goddess," we beg,
"Clean us, cure us,
unfold your wings

to lift the dams
before the flood.
Wash us with your might

to the brilliant place
where thunder
is the power

and women
shall wield it."

Florida Keys Authors

Get Published
Get Noticed
Get an Audience

It can all start here
Submit at Decimos.org

a publication of EPCO press

Holes in My Head
Sheri Lohr
Key West
Issue #14

I've taken several readings.
The results are clear:
From the outside looking in
    I can see air.

I have holes in my head.
No doubt
    there is matter leaking out.

The obvious, and ever more common questions:
    Why did I open the fridge?
        (Did I mean the cupboard?)
    What am I doing in this room?
    Where is that thing?
    Who is that person?
        (who seems to know me pretty well.)

I'm a sinking dinghy, and I'm dingy.

When did it get hard?
    Because I do remember
    when the words would pour.
And I couldn't stem the flood.
Now I wade into the spring
    and I'm stuck in mud.

Those thoughts and visions
    once flowed clear and sweet,

like the magic fountains of Florida.
And those springs too are today under threat.

So carry your signs and march if you will,
and mount your pulpit
        and rage at the sin
        of a species bound
        for a hell of its own devise.
Here's a surprise:
The planet doesn't care if we survive.

Because she is all one being,
        for a time, alive.
And we are the cells that briefly thrive
        then die.

And would her creator say to her
        "if thine hand offend thee, cut it off"?
And will she amputate us?
        like a girl who slices herself.

Our neighbor, Mars, they say,
        once had life-giving water
        but he boiled it all away.
Long before we came
        to take the blame.

Planets, stars, and galaxies
        have a mortal span.
So who would think an atom, or a cell,
        ever can
perceive the beginning,

or the end,
> of time?
And why should I expect
> to be forever agile in my mind?

The spring of my soul is a cenote.
A clear surface conceals the skulls
> of the sacrificed,
> and the hapless accidents.
In the deep, damp, dark
> are all the loves lost,
> and chances missed,
> and sweet memories gone dim,
> and even the pointless conflicts
>> that happened only yesterday.

So how should I recall
> why I came into this room?

Deaths and departures,
Friendships faded and failed,
Plans petered out,
> have all leaked through
> these holes
>> in my head.

And maybe my better stories have been said,
> my better lines read.

However,
> it is also true,
>> I'm not dead.

Worms on the Brain
William "Bucky" Montgomery
Key West
Issue #14

"Welcome to your new home, folks," Mr. Perkins, the dry, informal landlord stated as he let the elderly tenants in through the rickety front door. It was a welcome that sounded sincere. A bit patronizing, but sincere.

"It isn't our home. We're just renting," Homer groused in his usual sardonic tone. "And it smells like dirt in here."

"Don't you start," his wife Erma said, displaying a sharp eye.

Homer reluctantly responded to her warning, but managed to mumble, " I mean it. Dirt."

Mr. Perkins ran his finger across the windowsill and held it up toward them. "Clean as a whistle," he said. "The tenants here before you kept it up just fine. Despite their faults, they were clean."

"It's fine, Mr. Perkins," Erma replied with a weak smile. "Looks like whoever lived here before moved out in a hurry, though. Some of this furniture looks rather valuable."

"Well to be quite honest with you folks," Perkins explained, "They were crooks, the man and his wife. You would've never known it by looking at them. Sweet couple at first glance, from West Virginia, if I remember rightly. The furniture was probably stolen, or bought with stolen money, but the local police have no proof of that. So, now it's mine, or rather, yours, now that you're renting."

"It's nice," Homer mumbled. "For crook furniture..."

"Armed robbers, they were. First Nation Bank on the corner of Parker and Elm in town. Thousands of dollars."

"Oh, goodness. So they're in jail then?" Erma questioned.

"No ma'am. After they stashed the loot, seems that the fellow got greedy or jealous, and killed his wife, or something like that. It wasn't here, though. It was in town, late one night, after they had been drinking at a hotel lounge. It's been awhile now. He got caught right away. Died in prison the first week he was there, by the girl's cousin, so I guess they never got to spend their stolen loot."

"Shame."

"Serves them right, I s'pose. Wasn't a cordial man to begin with. He was facing life for previous crimes, with the chair at the end of the road for the murder of his poor wife," he said grimly. "But enough of that. I don't want you folks getting the feeling that this place is haunted or any such nonsense."

"Smells like dirt in here," Homer repeated with more vigor. "And worms."

"Pay him no mind, Mr. Perkins," Erma apologized. "Homer's not been the same, well, since the disease..."

Perkins nodded blankly, choosing politeness over curiosity. "Well," he said. "You've paid your first month's rent, but I still need your security deposit, and then I'll be on my way until next month. That's $450, right?

Erma opened her ratty purse with arthritic hands, retrieving a small roll of cash, wrapped with a fat rubber band. Reluctantly she held it out toward him, trying to smile and be thankful for the transaction, but her weary eyes revealed her true anxiety. "It's all there," she said to him. Every single penny that they had.

"Erma," Homer called from across the room, pointing at the floor near her feet. "I just saw one, right then. I saw the little devil stick its pointed, flat head right up out of the carpet, red as a beet, just like they did back at the apartment..."

"Stop it Homer. You know better."

"Looked right at me, Erma. Right at me. Dammit, we can't stay here. The worms are here, too. Place is infested with 'em."

Mr. Perkins was surveying the floor with a puzzled look on his face.

"If that's all, Mr. Perkins," Erma interjected, "we'd like to head on to bed now. Homer's tired. The rest of the furniture will be here in the morning , and we need to get our rest."

"I understand," he said, again with a slightly demeaning, patronizing tone that the middle-aged enjoyed speaking to the elderly. He pocketed the money, and within a few short minutes, he was gone.

Erma hobbled across the living room and eased into a dusty old antique armchair in the corner. It smelled like old wet newspapers and damp basement walls. She glanced at the thin, worn carpet and the torn, shabby curtains, and she put her face into her hands and began to cry.

Homer kept his vigil, crawling around the small house on his hand and knees, sniffing at the floor like a crazed bloodhound, rubbing his palms and gnarled knuckles across the threadbare carpet as if smoothing out lumps. Erma could hear him whispering angrily to himself about the cost of an exterminator.

"You realize, don't you, that we're stone cold broke? We can't afford the gas and electric, or even to have the water turned on, Homer." She watched him circle the room for some time, perhaps five entire laps. Her eyes were red from crying, and her voice was weak and shaky. "Not even enough for a decent dinner tonight."

Homer did not acknowledge her. He was too busy, hunting and hammering lightly on the floor with his fist whenever he spotted a worm moving along, making its burrow beneath the carpet. "There's a knot of the leathery bastards right there, wiggling and squiggling," he mumbled, pressing the flat beneath the dry-rotted weave with all his strength.

"Damn you, Homer," she hissed at him as she rose for bed. Her legs and hips ached horribly. "I thought we had left the worms behind."

Each morning Erma woke to the sound of her husband crawling about the house, cursing at the worm nests under the carpet, and each night she went to bed the same way. At least his mad obsession made him oblivious to the squalor and day-to-day suffering and misery that Erma was subjected to endure. They could not afford a telephone on their welfare checks, and even if they could, all their friends and family were dead or gone, so there was no one for them to call, for help or for company.

On rent day, the first of the month, the meager welfare money was gone, and Erma knew that Mr. Perkins would soon be by for his due. She went to the refrigerator, a nervous ulcer burning in her empty belly, and opened the door. A waft of soured milk washed past. The light bulb flickered and went out. Inside was mostly empty cartons and moldy tubs with bits and pieces of leftovers from the past month's slim pickings. She found half a stick of crumb-covered butter, and some onion skins, and having no other choice, she ate them.

"Erma! Come look! A whole heap of them in the corner here," Homer cried out from down the hall, almost excitedly.

Erma's spotted hands were trembling. She tried hard to keep control of her senses. Her stomach growled, and just then, in her delirium, her eyes began playing tricks on her. The room's light seemed to grow dimmer, as though a cloud had just passed before the sun.

Then, out of the corner of her eye, Erma noticed movement close to the floor, a slight, writhing wiggle. Startled by it, she quickly turned to focus on it, and there, by God, was one of Homer's blessed worms, a long, slick, reddish-brown creature, protruding up from a hole in the weave, dancing serpent-like. It was exactly as Homer had always described them to her over the years: at least a foot-and-a-half long, flat rather than cylindrical, and pointed at the foremost tip. It seemed to be watching her as she stared at it, then, in an instant, it disappeared when she blinked her eyes.

An illusion, she thought, shaking. She was covered with a cold sweat. She was afraid she was about to faint.

"There's some more, back here by the bookcase," Homer called.

Erma's face grew red, from her neck up to her wilted cheeks. He never tired. Ever. He was diligent on his idiotic quest, and now, his madness was becoming her own.

"Call the exterminator, Emma. Goddammit! Let's get rid of these goddamn worms once and for all!"

Erma stood suddenly, her chair crashing behind her, and without thinking, she seized the dull butcher knife from the drain board, and walked briskly through the dining room.

She saw him as she stormed around the corner, kneeling as always, the bones of his spine running a singular lumpy trail down the back of his yellow t-shirt, brom his baggy, stained boxers to his scraggly, sun-spotted scalp. "Got you!" he piped, smacking at the carpet with a rusty spatula, stirring up a small cloud of dust. "Aw, shit. Missed again."

Erma screamed in furious frustration, and fell to her knees at his side, burying the knife into the floor with all her feeble might. "If there's worms under this carpet," she shrieked madly, "I'll eat them! I swear I will eat them!"

Enraged to the point of recklessness, she shredded the dry-rotted weave with the knife over and over again, ripping and tearing at it ferociously with her left hand, filling the room with choking dust. "See Homer!?" she cried, coughing. "See? No worms! There ain't no worms under here! No worms! There's no worms! None! See? See?"

Homer had risen to his rug-chaffed knees, staring wide-eyed at the antics of his crazed wife. "How about...over there?"

Erma pulled at the carpet, staples popping like kernels of corn in a microwave, until her hands bled. "Nothing, you insane bastard!" she wailed "Now, for God's sakes, please shut up about the goddamn worms! Do you understand me, Homer? I mean, forever! There's NO WORMS!"

"No," he said plainly and matter-of-factly. "But there's...money."

It wasn't until she noticed the bills floating around the room, wreathed in the dust cloud, that Homer's statement finally registered in her ringing ears. They were mostly twenty's and fifty's, but there was noticeably many hundred dollar bills mingled in with them.

She stopped and stared, unable to draw a breath.

"You're right, though, Erma, you surely are," Homer admitted, pushing his way up to a stand. He kicked at a pile of shredded carpet. "There ain't no worms under there. I can see that now. There surely ain't a one..."

Erma was holding up two fistfuls of hundred dollar bills, eyes as round as sugar doughnuts. "I...I..." she could only say.

There was a knock at the door.

She dropped the cash, turning to see the familiar silhouette of Perkins through the dining room curtain, twitching impatiently on the front porch stoop.

"W-who's there?" she dallied.

"I think it's Per—"

"Shhh!" she hissed at her husband.

"Bill Perkins," he answered, trying to peer in through the cracked window. "Today's the first. Rent's due. That's $450."

Erma looked to Homer for any advice or direction or help, but he seemed to be oblivious, more interested with something on the ceiling.

"F-fine," she stuttered, fumbling nervously with her purse. She looked inside, even though she knew that it was empty.

"Everything okay in there?" Perkins called, jiggling the door handle.

Erma swallowed nervously. She stooped and seized a handful of cash from the floor and stuffed it into her purse. She gathered her wits as best she could, primped at her ratted hair for a few seconds, and strutted towards the door as if she were leaving for a Sunday stroll.

She cracked the door open no more than three inches, filling the gap with her face and body, so that the nosy landlord could not see beyond. And he was certainly trying. "Do you have change?" she asked as pleasantly as she was able.

"You don't look very well—"

"I am a peach," she responded abruptly and displayed the sharp eye usually reserved for her twit of a husband. They stood there for a moment, eye to eye.

"Yes," he finally succumbed. "I have change."

"Here's five hundred," she said, pulling her hand from her purse and through the narrow opening at the door jam.

Perkins brow was taut. "I'm embarrassed to admit that I'm a little surprised you have your rent today. I was a bit worried you couldn't pay..."

"We can be resourceful if need be, Mr. Perkins," she chided, trying not to cough from the cloud of incapacitating dust. "And speaking of money, Mr. Perkins," she asked, "About those two who lived here before us..."

"The bank robbers?"

"Fascinating story," she chimed. "How much money did they get away with? Exactly?"

"Bank said $200,000, but there's no telling really," he replied, pocketing his cash. "They were gamblers, the two of them. Probably lost every nickel of it."

"Shame, shame."

"They lived up in Jackson after they left here. Probably took it with them. Never found a single dollar bill around this property, and believe me, we searched every inch."

"That's too bad," Erma said. "It really is. Money like that don't come around to deserving folk very often."

"Surely don't, Erma," Mr. Perkins said, his shoes clunking down the front porch steps. He opened his car door, stopped and called to her, just before she closed the door, "Hey, Erma!"

"Y-yes, Mr. Perkins?"

"If you find that treasure you'd be sure and let the authorities know, now wouldn't you? You'd call me?"

"Well..."

"Just kidding!" he laughed. "Have a good day now. See you the first of next month. Tell Homer I said hey."

Erma was smiling ear to ear as she watched his car pull away. She spun as gaily as a schoolgirl, eyeing the treasure strewn across the disarrayed floor. No more ice cold nights. No more ragged clothes. No more going hungry, ever again. Life...was going to change for them. "We're rich, Homer," she said. "My prayers have been answered. We are rich. All our problems are finally over!"

Homer was preoccupied right then, laying up, ear against the wall, listening intently. He nodded at her. "Good. Good. We can afford an exterminator then," he replied crossly. "I think these walls are infested with snakes!"

Support the Literary Arts of the Keys

Advertise in Decimos

BOOKER advertising

info@BookerAdvertising.com
305-395-7622

Plead
Vinny Scotts
Key West
Issue #15

Hot air came from those who packed the room,
My heart was visibly racing though my suit.

The whispering ceased from the audience,
As an officer's shoes tapped on the wooden floor,
In his scarred hand, my verdict.

The judge puts her glasses on,
My lawyer tightens his grip on my shoulder.
For the first time in weeks,
Dead silence.
A juror swallows.

I had the case,
I knew I won.
I'll return to my wife,
And we'll leave this wretched town.

My investment in law paid off,
I knew this when the judge's eyes read the page over again.
Years of schooling and work granted me this,
My freedom.

New York was calling my name,
Perhaps a child as well.
I winked at my wife as the judge began to read.

"The jury hereby declares Mr. Mathews guilty in the first degree murder of Casey Nolan"
I was over.

Gangus Hausenfluck
Jelena Sanchez
Key West
Issue #15

The camera is laying on the ground,

It tilts up, making all look profound.

The subject's a boy, small but now seems

So great he could tear the world to seams.

The once skinny boy is now a god,

Those in his presence must stare in awe.

He points to the skyline, his large hand

Shows the way towards a new promise land.

Hausenfluck towers above us all,

When he speaks he spits, 'tis our rainfall.

But all is not as well as we've said,

Our lord is great but fills us with dread.

We pray to him and call him our lord,

But he his a threat and nothing more.

We fear this man, deep down we all know

One wrong move and he'll go sicko mode.

Heist by the Local Dinosaur
Christina Tong
Key West
Issue #15

There in my bedroom there's my bed, obviously. On it, my blanket is twists like a volcano, and my stuffed animals huddle against my pillow and the wall. Near the window is my reading tent and an overflowing basket of books next to it. My reading buddy, Buffy the Brontosaurus, is probably sleeping inside. There's a fuzzy rug in the middle of my room and an almost finished jigsaw puzzle also on the floor. I'm at my desk. It's wooden and stained with paint and sharpie ink. A sticker of dinosaurs marching is stuck on.

I spin in my rolly chair before turning back to my drawing. My pencil lead snaps as I trace a curve, and I fling it across my room.

A dumb pencil! It'll never make it to college.

I'm frustrated, so I head to the refrigerator for juice. I swing open my door and slip on my dinosaur claw slippers, already tasting the sweet and tangy orange-pineapple in my mouth. The door of my parents' room swings open too.

Mom walks out.

"Annie," she says, "do you know where the money went?"

"What money?" I ask.

"The money that was in the bathroom, inside the bathtub. I asked

Mit, but he doesn't know," she explains. My mind flashes to that night, weeks ago. Should I tell her?

It's a mostly uneventful night. Mit takes over the bathroom, shoving me out and giving me only my toothbrush. Our parents are at work, so this is my weapon to fend off potential robbers? Why not at least the snorkel under the sink? I'm not sure if me in my dinosaur onesie will be enough to scare them off.

I go to the bad bathroom at the other side of the house to brush my teeth. In front of the mirror, I use my fingers to press my front teeth into a straight line, imagining the day I'll get braces. Mom said not until middle school, and that's way far off.

I unhood, no longer a dinosaur. I use Mom's hairbrush to brush my hair then spot something.

The bathtub! It's one of those tubs connected to the walls. On the bathtub's side that shows, plastic panels had fallen in. So gaps to the inside of the tub let me see a cement ground, large pipes, and something under those pipes . . .

I kneel on the floor and stick my hand in. I fish out a plastic bag. I examine the contents and decide that a load of money of this amount has no right being kept in the bathroom. Especially in such a not-so-obvious-yet-obvious place!

Plus, it would be funny if I moved it.

Tom and Jerry play in the background, a infinite game of chase and silliness, as I race across the house. Mit is still singing in the shower, meaning there's some time before he's done. I nearly slam open the sliding closet door in Mit's room before I bury the money under black garbage bags, full of his old clothes.

The money is safest this way. Mit's closet is somewhere no one ever looks in, not even Mit. Instead, he uses the dresser next to it.

I shut the door, and my reflection stares at me. It gives me a wink and pulls my hood back on.

I hop to my room and leap on my bed, throwing open a book and giving it a good glare as Mit opens the bathroom door. He doesn't even glance at me before entering his room. If he did, he'd know something's up, since I only ever read in my tent.

CLICK! Mom's loud snap makes me blink like someone just threw water in my face. I grab my head and steady myself.

"What?" I ask. "Oh, a bathtub is a bad place to put money. Why would you do that?"

"Annie, it was to hide the money. Did you take it?"

"What do mean, hide it?" Mom's being perplexicating. "What happened to the bank?"

"I was too busy. I was going to put it in the bank the next day."

"Oh," I reply dumbly. No, not dumb. What I did was smart.

Key West Island Books
513 Fleming St.
Old Town, Key West

Local Authors
Rare Books
Best Sellers
New and Used

KWIslandBooks.com
facebook.com/KWIslandBooks

I lead Mom to my brother's bedroom, where I bang on the door.

"WHAT!?"

"OPEN YOUR DOOR!"

We go into Mit's room and I slide the closet door open. I dig for the money, and hold it up like the hero I am.

Mom facepalms and Mit rolls his eyes.

I ask my mother in a sweet voice, "are you mad at me?"

"No, just- just don't do that again." She replies and takes the money.

"Why did you try to frame me?" Mit demands.

"Ummm . . ." I shrug and go back to my room. Mit shouts after me, complaining about that time I put toothpaste Oreos on the kitchen counter and wrote a note saying it was from him. I shut the door and yell, "dinosaurs can do whatever they want!"

Decimos - We Say
Advertising Price Sheet

1/4 page = $150/issue (3 months)
Full Page = $500/issue (3 months)

Decimos - We Say is a quarterly magazine. Ads purchased will run in print & digital version as well as on our website for the duration of the issue.

For more info:
JD Adler at contact@epcopress.com

Plover Promise
P Patten Tiffany
Key West
Issue #16

Oh to be a plover
skittering across
sugar-white sand
on Pensacola Beach

snatching juicy bits
of sea life
along white froth
shore's edge

telling an ancient story
on spindly legs
down two three
back two three

just beyond dunes'
bowing sea oats
where we watch
envious

of the energy
and purpose
freedom to fly
transfixed by the dance

A LITTLE PAIN IN THE BUTT NEVER HURT ANYONE
Alexandra Hope
Key West
Issue #16

Florida summer has arrived and with it the suffocating heat. I am sweating and hot after only one lap around the block with the dogs. We head back inside where I can hide best from the blazing sun. Trying to cool off, I plop down to the tile floor sitting on my butt with legs outstretched in front of me. My tailbone begins to protest with a dull familiar ache. A sledding accident, from my childhood, is the culprit of my discomfort and I can't help but smile wishing I could once again feel the icy wind on my face as I raced down the snow-covered hill.

"Mom, my gloves are still wet!" I yell.

"Just use a pair of socks instead - - and grab some for your brothers too!" she shouts back.

Pouting, I run and grab a pair of socks, choosing the ones with the least number of holes for myself. Hurrying back, I toss on my ugly yellow coat as I shove my feet into snow boots that are a size too big. My brothers are crowded next to me yanking and tugging at their own snow gear. We are all clad in an assortment of thrift store finds and hand-me-downs from more well-to-do cousins. Turner, my brother, hates second-hand clothing and scowls as he tucks his pants into hot pink snow boots. I look over and giggle at the sight of Jake, my youngest brother. He resembles a fat little cardinal in his red coat and chubby pink cheeks.

"Come on guys! They are probably waiting for us already!" Turner grumbles.

We head out the door hollering goodbyes to our mother and promises that we will come back if we get too cold. Waiting, are our neighborhood friends Ross and Shawn. They are brothers who live across the street and who we spend most of our free time with. Shawn is the older of the two with dark black hair and skinny as a rail. His younger brother Ross has slightly lighter hair and is just as skinny. They are bundled up and wearing real snow gloves, unlike my brothers and me. They are also dressed in proper fitting snowsuits.

Grabbing our snow saucers and sleds, we head through shin-deep snow to the "Hill". The Hill is steep, even as an adult I can acknowledge this as true. Past rainstorms have created a crack like line down its center, halfway down a large rock protrudes from the ground. This rock is our pride and joy. We have used the rock to our advantage after failing to uproot it out of our path. Instead, we have packed snow around the stones and added a thick layer on top for padding creating a ramp Tony Hawk would be proud of. We have spent days manipulating the snow in the crack to create our own version of an Olympic bobsled luge track that heads in a straight line right for the rock jump.

We troop down the Hill single file, oldest to youngest, with faces set in serious determination. Today, there will be no playing around with haphazard sledding escapades or snowball fights. No sir. We are on a mission to try out our jump in all its glory. Of course, we have done a few test runs when the jump was just a little lump protruding from our path and weighted down sleds empty of its rider once it arose higher than our waist. Today will be the day of reckoning, and we will ride and conquer the white monster in all its glory.

"It looks so cool!" Shawn declares as if any of us are having doubts about such an obvious fact.

"Who's going first?" says Turner, always the cautious one of the group.

"The oldest should do it," Ross states matter-of-factly.

Glancing down the Hill, my eyes are drawn to the snow-slicked rock rising out of the ground like a small igloo. I am the only girl in our little neighborhood gang and know this is my chance to beat the boys at something. Tugging my knit snow cap firmly down over my ears I loudly proclaim, "I will do it". The boys all turn to look at me, eyes bright with excitement in anticipation of my probable crash.

"But you're the girl, and not the oldest" Jake logically remarks.

"Who cares, plus I'm the second oldest anyhow" I shoot back.

"Fine, just let her do it" Shawn, the leader of our group, declares.

We debate what sled should be used for more than ten minutes, finally deciding upon Shawn's lime green racer that has built-in footrests and handles. I soon realize this ends up being a poor choice. The area made to rest one's foot is molded out of rigid plastic and into sharp hard points on each side. This happens to be a convenient feature when sliding gently down a hill with your whole body firmly seated and not flying a foot above the sled.

Grasping the handles with my sock covered hands, I plant myself confidently in the seat and position my feet in the dedicated spot. My heart starts to pound in my chest and I force myself to relax. Looking to my right I see Ross wiping his runny nose on his coat sleeve and Turner kicking at the snow with the pink tip of his boot. Jake stands behind me ready for Shawn's signal to give me a hearty push.

"You ready?" Jake asks.

"Yup!" I say with far more confidence than I'm feeling.

With that Shawn lifts both of his skinny arms above the pompom on his hat. Looking me in the eyes, he gives a little nod and shouts… "Ready… Set… One… Two… Three… GO!" and drops his arms with an exaggerated flourish.

My sled moves forward slowly at first. Jake pushes my back, hard, to remedy my slow start. Momentum begins to take over with the help of gravity pulling my sled down towards my pending victory. I can feel the sting of cold winter air on my face as I slide closer and closer to the snow-covered rock. Sunlight catches in the wide arc of snow spraying out from under my sled as I whiz past the rays shooting through the tree line. I sense my brothers running close behind me ready to be there as witness to my success or failure. Squinting I search in front of me for the jump and see it looming ahead. It seems to have grown higher since I set off down the Hill to tackle its might. My fingers grow damp inside my socks, and I scrunch my toes in the too big boots as if I can use them to hold tighter to the sled.

In seconds I am within feet of the jump. I feel my body stiffen as the sled's nose hits the ramp base. Suddenly I am in the air flying above the lime green sled that had been holding me safely just a moment ago. The white ground sparkles brightly as I begin to fall back down to earth. I don't feel too concerned since snow is soft and I should land neatly in a pile of it, and so I relax enough to let my body land as gravity intends.

Wham!! Snow sprays around me as my body hits, not only the ground but the sled as well. Red hot pain shoots up my backside as my poor rear-end lands square on the sleds perfectly sharpened edged of the footrest. No pillow like snowy landing for me. Oh, no sir. Instead, I have somehow flown up and over the jump into the air crashing right back down on the sled in the worst possible way. I screech in pain and roll onto my stomach, clutching at my backside.

"Hope! You ok!" Shawn says excitedly.

"I knew you would crash!" Turner worriedly cries.

"That was so cool!" Jake and Ross exclaim in unison.

I lay in the cold snow with my brothers and friends hovering around me. Groaning I hobble to my feet. "Who's next?" I smile.

I limped for a month after that snow day, having most likely fractured my tail bone. It still bothers me twenty some years later. Sighing I stand up and walk to the bathroom where I keep the Tylenol. Popping two in my mouth, I swallow them down with a gulp of water. Despite my discomfort, I am thankful for little reminders of my happy youth. Glancing up, I stare at my reflection in the mirror and think to myself that A little pain in the butt never hurt anyone, especially when it brings a smile to your face.

The X News Hour
Sunday Mornings 10am-12pm
104.9 the X
XKeyWest.com

An Unusual Hour of News You Can Use

EDITORIAL BOARD

EDGARDO ALVARADO-VÁZQUEZ
I was born and raised in Bayamón, Puerto Rico. In 1995 I arrived in Key West with my husband Stephen and my furry family. The Key West Writers Guild and the Key West Poetry Guild are my soul's houses. In 2014 I was awarded the Anne McKee Foundation grant to publish my first novel, The Funerals of Key West. In 2016 I was awarded a second grant to publish my poetry book, Don't Read This Poetry Book; that year I was recognized by the foundation with the Richard Heyman award for poetry. I am working on my second novel.

VICKI BOGUSZEWSKI
holds a Masters of Public Health from Florida International University and a Bachelor Art's in Cultural Anthropology from Temple University. Her career as a poet began in the second grade, c. spring 1979, in Sicklerville, NJ, with a recitation of Shel Silverstein's poem, "Sick." Her first collection of original art & poetry, Mesource, was self-published on local Sea Story Press in 2008. Her work was included in the Key West Poetry Guild's 2012 Anthology; Key West, I Love You. She is a longstanding member of the Guild, having joined their ranks as a young poet in 1996, and sits on the Coordinating Committee as the Corresponding Secretary. In 2014 she initiated a celebration of Black American Poetry hosted and celebrated by the Guild every February. She was the lead judge for the 2015 Tennessee William's Birthday Celebration Poetry Contest.

KALO CLARKE
I don't remember writing; I don't remember not writing. I do remember parental orders not to write on walls. Over the years I've taught writing– all kinds of writing from technical to creative– in university classrooms, in board rooms, on TV, and on line. I'm the former Director of Northeastern University's Writing Center, a published poet, a grant writer, co-founder of several literary magazines, and judge for many writing contests.

FLOWER CONROY
is the author of Facts About Snakes & Hearts, winner of Heavy Feather Press' Chapbook Contest; The Awful Suicidal Swans; and Escape to Nowhere. Her poetry's been nominated for Best of the Net, Best New Poets and Pushcart Prizes and has won Radar Poetry's first annual Coniston Prize, the Key West Tennessee Williams Poetry Contest and the Richard Heyman Award. She is a scholarship recipient of Bread Loaf, Squaw Valley, Napa Valley and the Key West Literary Seminar. She is the former Poet Laureate of Key West.

JD ADLER
published his first poem for $5 at the age of 16. At 19, he dropped out of college (the first time) and created an arts guild with his friends, including publishing his first literature magazine. Eventually JD completed several degrees while traveling America. He has developed publication projects for universities, non-profits and small business, self-published 5 books, the occassional work of freelance journalism, and once wrote and co-produced a tv pilot. His favorite project was a volunteer workshop teaching kids to write short stories, then publishing the results in an anthology. To see the face of a writer first published is to look on pure joy.

www.ingramcontent.com/pod-product-compliance
Lightning Source LLC
Chambersburg PA
CBHW070442010526
44118CB00014B/2161